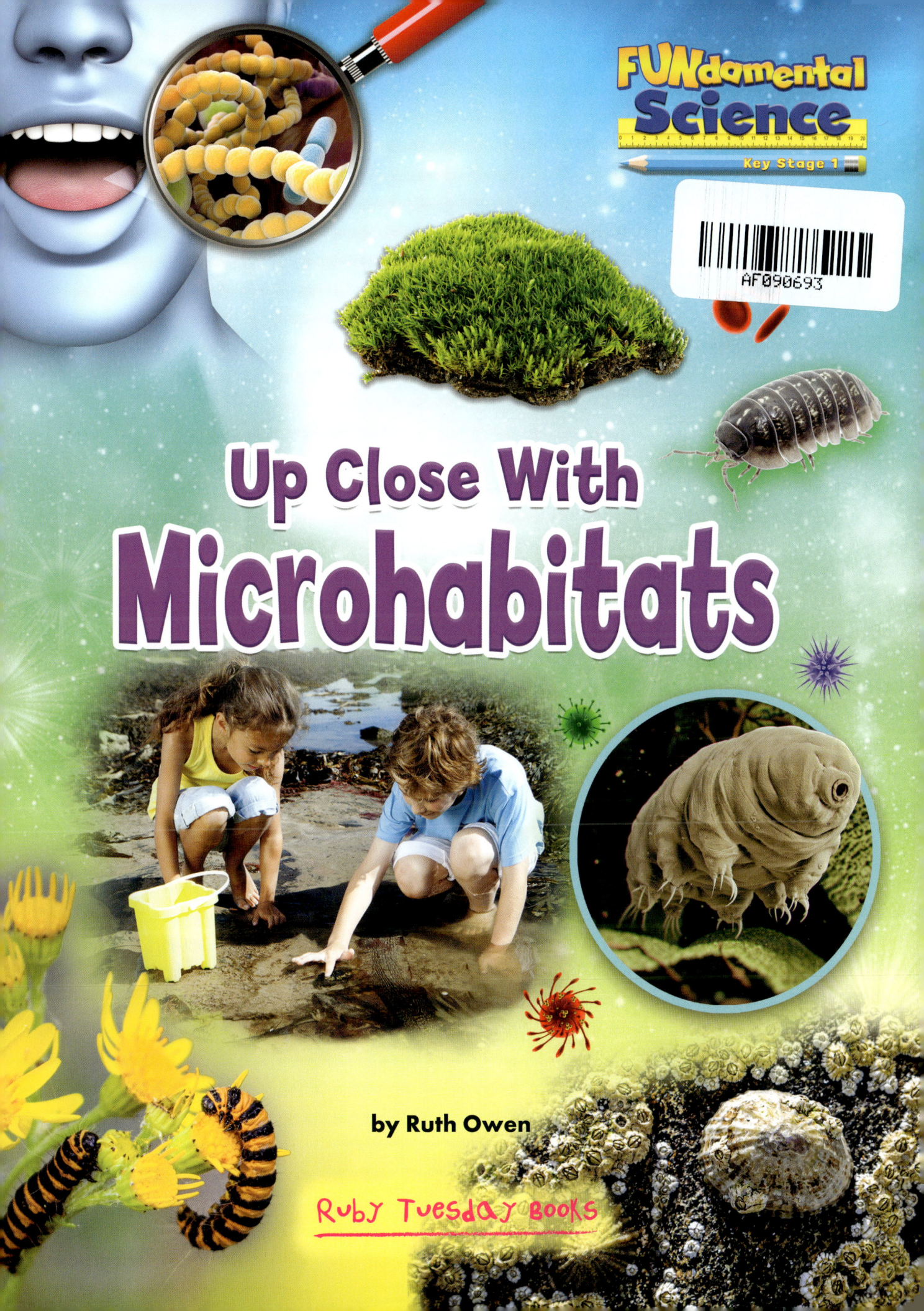

Published in 2022 by Ruby Tuesday Books Ltd.

Copyright © 2022 Ruby Tuesday Books Ltd.

All rights reserved. No part of this publication may be reproduced in whole or in part, stored in any retrieval system, or transmitted in any form or by any means, electronic, mechanical, photocopying, recording, or otherwise, without written permission from the publisher.

Editor: Mark J. Sachner
Designer: Emma Randall
Production: John Lingham

Photo credits:
Creative Commons: 23 (Marek Mis); Nature Picture Library: 17C (Kim Taylor), 27B (Tony Wu); NOAA: 29B (Craig Smith); OET/NOAA: 27C, 28T; Greg Rouse: 28B, 29T; Science Photo Library: 12B (Eye of Science), 21 (Eye of Science), 22B (Frank Fox), 31C (Steve Gschmeissner); Shutterstock: Cover (Tatiana Shepeleva/Ihor Hvozdetskyi/Vector Tradition/Cloudpost/Air Images/3Dstock/Starsphinx/Melanie Hobson), 4T (Nattapol Sritongcom), 4B (Wolf Avni), 5T (Willyam Bradberry), 5C (Rob Dun), 5B (Erni), 6 (Dietmar Rauscher/Steve Cymro/Erni/tchara/MagicBones/steshs), 7 (Artiste2d3d/Cjansuebsri/Eric Isselee/anat chant), 8T (grey_and), 8BL (Vita Serendipity), 8BR (Holger Kirk), 9T (Catherine Eckert), 9C (smspsy), 9B (Reinier Blok), 10T (skippy666), 10B (Photo Fun), 11T (Eric Isselee), 11B, 12T (Evan Lorne), 13T (Kaleb Kroetsch), 13B (udomsook), 14L (enterphoto/grafvision/Chris Brignell/pzaxe), 14R (Alex Buess), 15T (pzaxe/anat chant/Hintau Aliaksei), 15B (Matauw/Vitalii Hulai), 16T (Andres Sonne), 16B (Coulanges), 17T (Henrik Larsson), 17B (Ernie Cooper), 18T (Julie Vader), 18B (Ian Peter Morton), 19 (Faris Fitrianto/Tom Meaker/Davydenko Yuliia), 20 (3Dstock), 22T (Soloviova Liudmyla), 24 (Christopher Meder/Guy Cowdry/Macrovector), 25T (Melanie Hobson), 25B (tartmany), 26 (Maui Topical Images), 27T (Dmitry Demkin/Alexander Raths/pan demin/zcw/Ekaterina Semenets), 30TL (Anatoliy Karlyuk), 30TR (Prostock Studio), 30B (Valentina Antuganova), 31T (Kalcutta/Ronnachai Palas), 31B (Maen CG).

British Library Cataloguing in Publication Data (CIP) is available for this title.

ISBN 978-1-78856-204-1

Printed in Poland by L&C Printing Group

www.rubytuesdaybooks.com

Contents

What Is a Habitat? 4
What Is a Microhabitat? 6
Living on a Cabbage 8
Meet Some Woodlice 10
In the Compost Heap 12
Compost Heap Minibeasts 14
Life Under a Log 16
Life on a Log 18
Meet the Tiny Tardigrades 20
A Puddle Microhabitat 22
Life on a Rock 24
When a Whale Falls 26
Life on a Skeleton 28
You Are the Microhabitat! 30
Glossary, Index, Answers 32

Words shown in **bold** in the text are explained in the glossary.

The download button shows there are free worksheets or other resources available. Go to:
www.rubytuesdaybooks.com/scienceKS1

What Is a Habitat?

A garden, a grassland, the ocean or a woodland are all types of **habitats**.

A habitat is a natural **environment** where a living thing, such as a plant or animal, normally lives.

A plant needs soil to grow. It also needs air, sunshine and water.

Living things get everything they need to survive from their habitat.

Let's Talk

Look at the pictures. What are the animals getting from their habitat?

(The answers are at the bottom of page 5.)

Grassland habitat

Ocean habitat

Woodland habitat

Garden habitat

Answers: Water, food (berries), a mate to have young with and a home (a squirrel's drey, or nest). A home protects an animal from weather and predators that want to eat it. It's also a place to raise young.

What Is a Microhabitat?

The word "micro" means very small. A microhabitat is a very small habitat.

A habitat, such as a garden, may have lots of microhabitats.

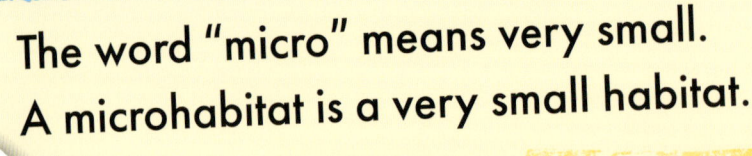

A spider lives in the bush.

A mouse lives in the shed.

A mole lives under the grass.

Ants live under the bricks.

A snail lives on a plant.

The ground beneath a rock is a type of microhabitat.

Under a rock it is dark and **damp**. Tiny animals that like this kind of environment make it their home.

Millipede

Slug

Centipede

Let's Explore!

Can you find some microhabitats in your garden or school playground?

Gather your equipment:
- A notebook and pen

1. Begin by exploring the garden or playground.

Do you see any places that could be microhabitats?

2. Write down your ideas. For example: some bricks, flowerpots or an old log.

3. Now choose a microhabitat to investigate. Remember! You may be disturbing the home of some tiny animals. Be very careful when you lift or move any item.

What do you observe in the microhabitat?

Did you spot any living things? What did they do? Record your observations.

4. Now investigate a different microhabitat and compare it to the first one.

How are the two microhabitats alike? How are they different?

7

Living on a Cabbage

In a vegetable garden, a cabbage can become a microhabitat.

A cabbage white butterfly lays up to 100 tiny eggs on the cabbage. Why?

Cabbage

Cabbage white butterfly

Eggs

Because cabbage leaves are her caterpillars' favourite food!

After one week, a tiny caterpillar hatches from each egg.

The caterpillars eat cabbage and grow bigger and bigger.

The cabbage microhabitat is their home and their food!

After four weeks, each caterpillar becomes a **pupa**. Then it changes into a butterfly.

Meet Some Woodlice

If you look under some damp leaves or a rock, you might find lots of woodlice.

Long ago, these tiny animals lived in water.

Over millions of years, they **adapted** to live on land.

Dead leaf

Woodlouse

Woodlice eat rotting leaves and other bits of dead plants.

10

Woodlice still need water to breathe.

Parts for breathing are under here.

They have body parts that take **oxygen** out of tiny amounts of water.

That's why they live in microhabitats that are very damp.

Woodlice Microhabitats

Let's Talk

Woodlice also choose dark places to live. Why?
(The answer is on page 32.)

In the Compost Heap

A compost heap is a type of microhabitat. It is home to millions of living things.

Compost heap

A rotting leaf

Microbes

Microbes are so small they can only be seen with a microscope.

Tiny **microbes** live in compost heaps.

They help turn the vegetable peelings and other waste into new soil.

Fungus

Different types of **fungi** live in a compost heap.

They spread thin, white threads called mycelium through the compost.

Mycelium

The mycelium feed on the plant waste and help to break it down.

Compost Heap Minibeasts

A compost heap provides a home and food for lots of animals.

These minibeasts eat rotting plants in a compost heap.

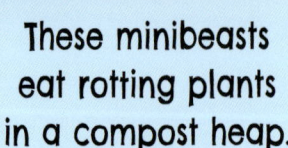

Millipede

Snail

Slug

Woodlice

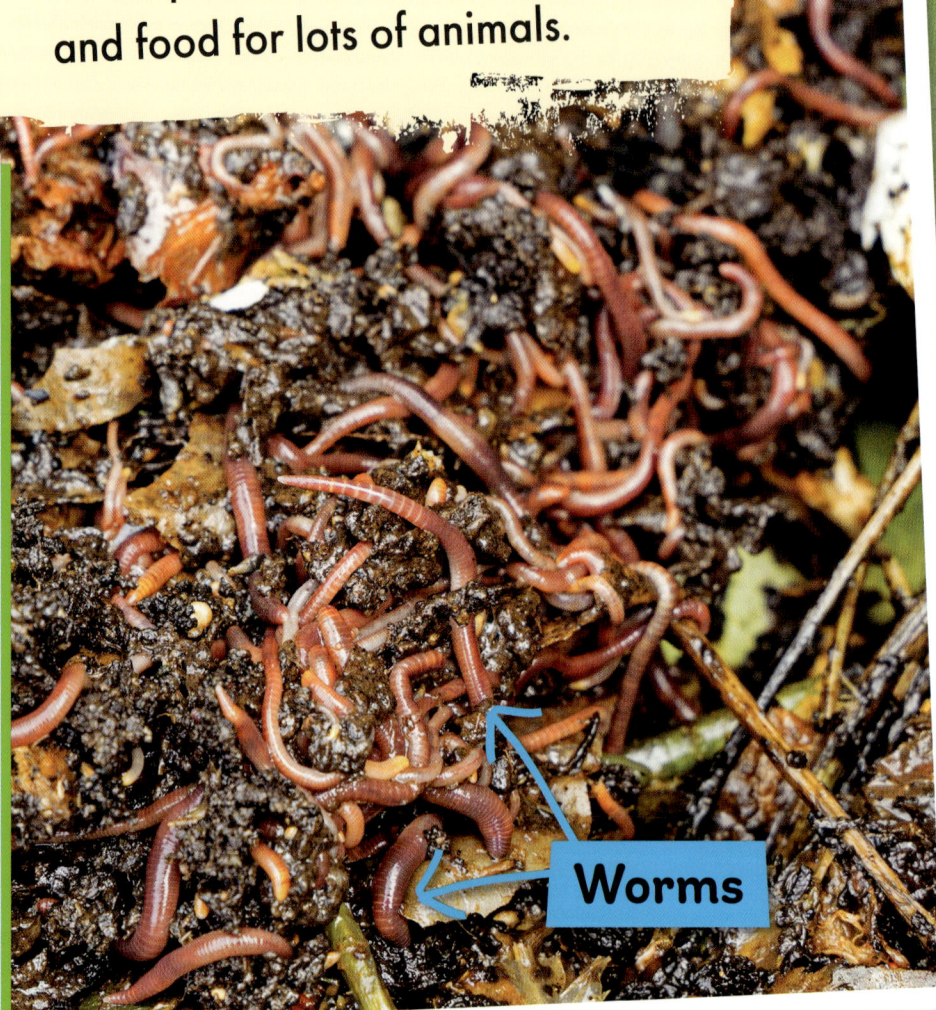

Worms

Worms and millipedes eat the waste in a compost heap.

Their poo becomes part of the compost.

Centipedes hunt for woodlice, worms and insects in a compost heap.

A Compost Heap Food Chain

Plant waste   Woodlouse   Centipede   Toad

The arrows mean eaten by

Grass snake eggs

Toads and grass snakes take shelter in this microhabitat.

A grass snake may lay her eggs in the compost heap. The heat from the rotting plants keeps the eggs warm.

Grass snake

15

Life Under a Log

When a tree dies, its trunk and branches become a microhabitat.

Lots of minibeasts live under rotting logs. You might spot ants, centipedes, millipedes, slugs, spiders, woodlice and worms.

Newt

Newts hide under logs and hunt for the minibeasts that live there.

Stag beetles

Female

Male

A stag beetle lays her eggs in the soil beneath a log.

A larva eating wood

A **larva** hatches from each egg and feeds on the rotting wood.

Be a Scientist!

What lives under a rotting log?

Gather your equipment:
- A hand lens or magnifying glass
- A small jar
- A spoon and paintbrush
- A notebook and pen

What animals do you see? Do you see anything that could be food for the animals beneath the log?

1. In a garden, park or woodland, look for a rotting log that's small enough to roll.

2. Slowly and carefully roll the log away from you. Be ready to spot minibeasts as soon as you move the log!

3. Use the spoon or paintbrush to gently scoop any animal you want to study into your jar. Do not touch the animal with your hands.

4. Record your observations in your notebook.

5. Carefully roll the log back into its starting position. Gently tip any animals from your jar next to the log and let them crawl back to their home.

A woodlouse spider eating a woodlouse

Life on a Log

The outside of a rotting log can become a microhabitat.

Fungus

Fungi grow on the log and feed on the dead wood.

Colourful lichens

Plant-like living things called lichens live on old branches and tree stumps.

Moss

Moss plants grow on a log like a soft, green carpet.

Each tiny plant is just a single stem and some leaves.

Moss plants don't have roots. Their leaves soak up rainwater from the log.

Be a Scientist!

What happens to moss if it doesn't rain?

Gather your equipment:
- A shallow dish
- A notebook and pen
- A tablespoon
- Some water

1. In a garden, park or woodland, collect a small clump of moss about the size of an egg.

2. Put the moss into the dish and place the dish on a sunny windowsill for two weeks.

What do you observe happening to the moss? Record your observations in your notebook.

3. After two weeks, gently sprinkle the moss with 4 tablespoons of water.

What do you think will happen now? Write your prediction in your notebook.

4. Check the moss after 12 hours.

What is happening? Did your prediction match what happened?

(There are some answers at the bottom of the page.)

Answers: The moss probably became very dry. It may also have changed colour. But the little plants didn't die. Once the plants were given water, their leaves soaked it up. The moss became damp and bright green again.

19

Meet the Tiny Tardigrades

A clump of moss on a log is home to **microscopic** animals called tardigrades.

Tardigrade

They live in tiny amounts of water on the moss.

Hooked claws

Sucker-like mouth

8 legs

Tardigrades suck juices from the moss.

If no rain falls, the moss dries up.

The tiny tardigrades dry up, too.

Tun

A dried-up tardigrade is called a tun. It can stay this way for years and years.

Once it rains, the moss soaks up water.

The tardigrades take in water, too, and start moving around again!

A Puddle Microhabitat

A puddle may only look like some muddy water. But it can be a microhabitat.

Puddle

Microscopic swimming animals called rotifers live in puddles.

They feed on microbes, tiny bits of plants and other microscopic animals.

Rotifer

Let's Talk

What do you think happens to a rotifer if its puddle home dries up?

(The answer is on page 32.)

Microscopic water fleas also live in puddles.

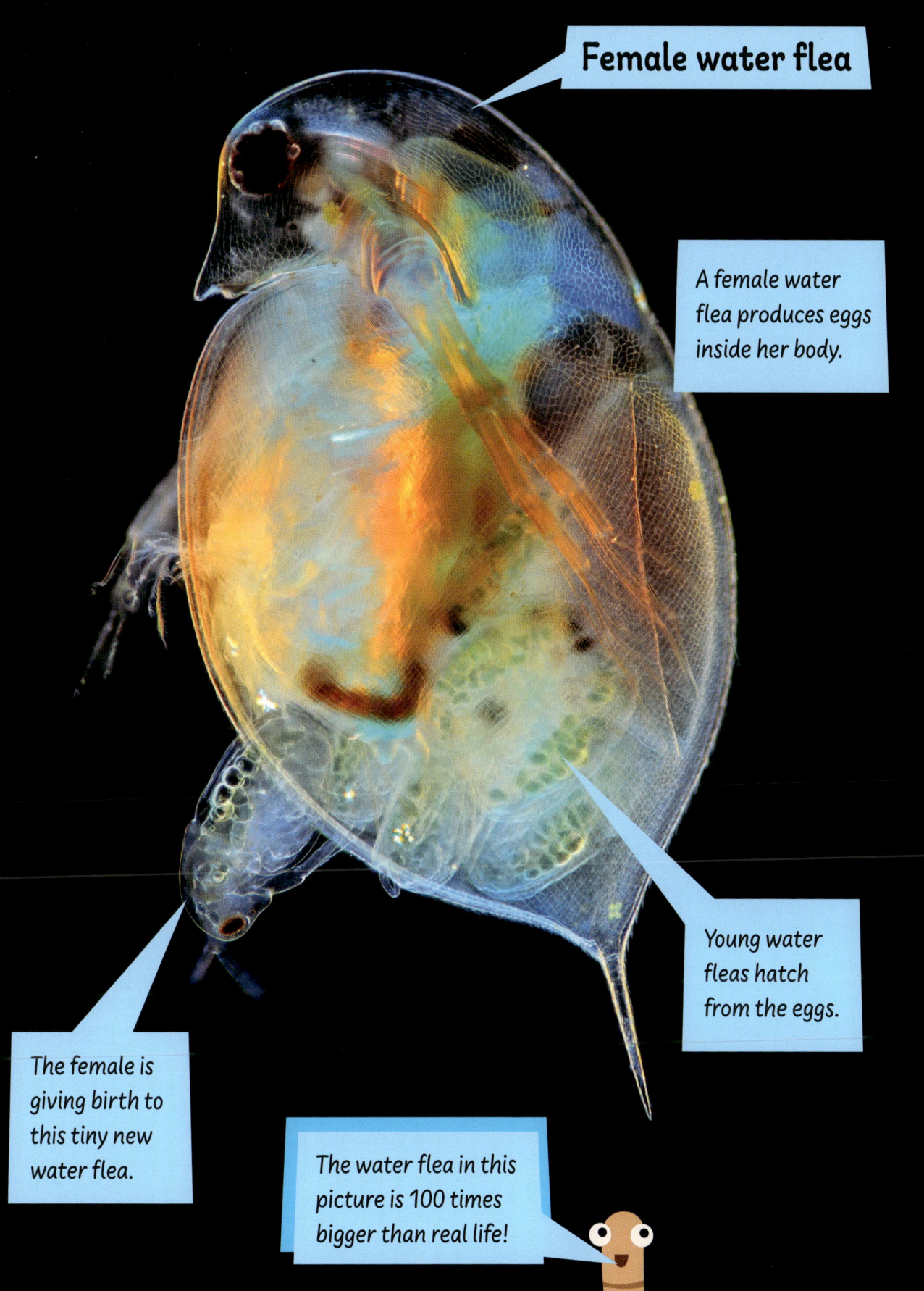

Female water flea

A female water flea produces eggs inside her body.

Young water fleas hatch from the eggs.

The female is giving birth to this tiny new water flea.

The water flea in this picture is 100 times bigger than real life!

Life on a Rock

On a beach, you might find a rock pool.

Seaweed clings to the rocks.

Microscopic animals called plankton live in the water.

Rock pool

And in a rock pool, you might find a rock that's a whole microhabitat.

24

Tiny animals called barnacles and limpets live on the rock.

A limpet has its own spot on a rock that is its home. It only leaves this spot to find seaweed to eat.

Limpet

Barnacles

Trap doors

Barnacles

When water covers the rock, each barnacle opens its tiny trap doors.

Then it grabs plankton from the water with its legs.

25

When a Whale Falls

The ocean is home to lots of different microhabitats.

When a whale dies, its giant body falls to the seabed.

Then it becomes a microhabitat known as a "whale fall".

Fish, eels, octopuses, lobsters, sea cucumbers, clams, giant isopods and other animals quickly gather.

Eel

Lobster

Octopus

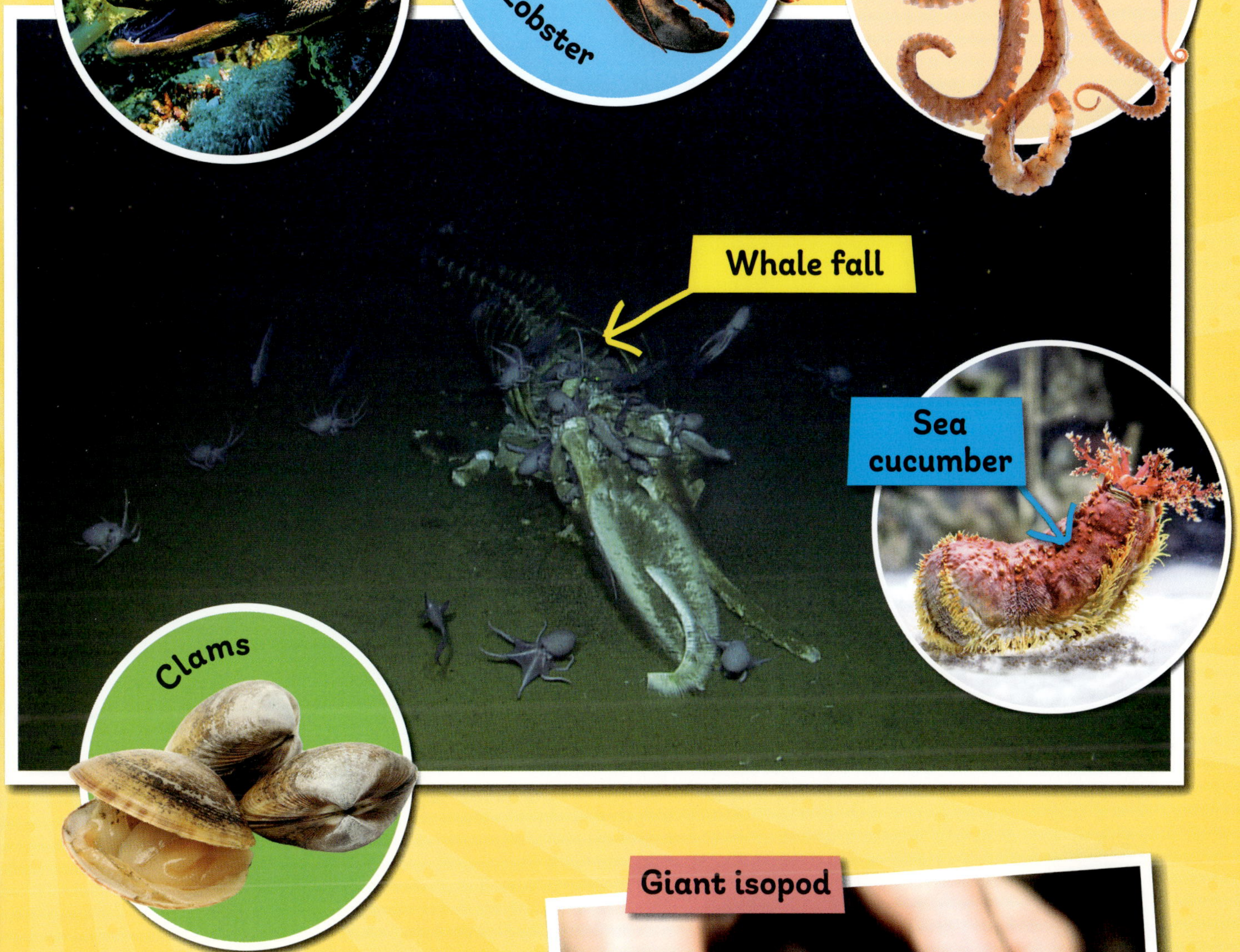

Whale fall

Sea cucumber

Clams

Giant isopod

The animals live around the whale's body, feeding on its skin, muscles and fat.

Giant isopods live at the bottom of the ocean. They are relatives of woodlice.

Life on a Skeleton

For up to 10 years, lots of animals feed on the whale fall.

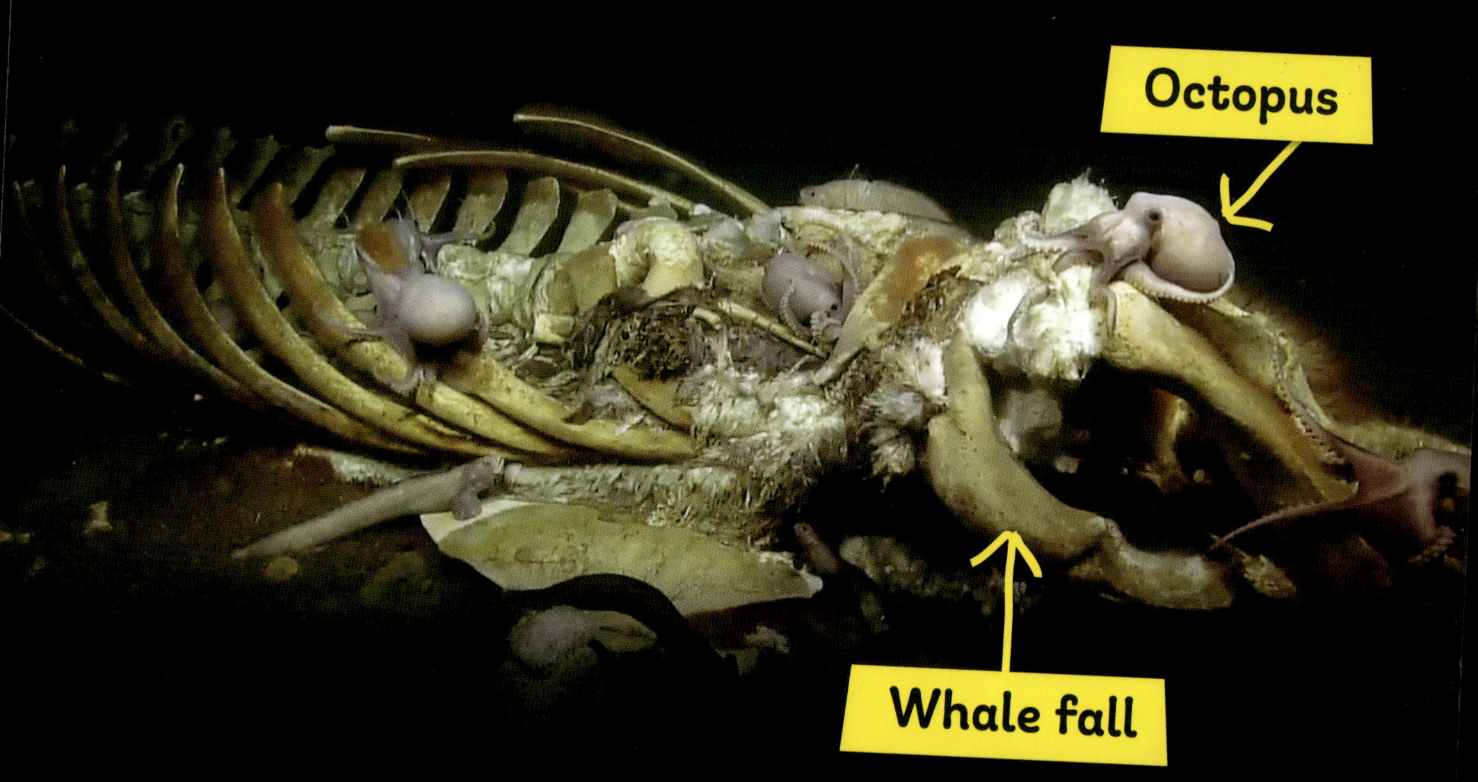

Octopus

Whale fall

When all that's left is bone, the bone-eating worms get to work.

Worms

Bone-eating worm

The bone-eating worms have root-like parts that tunnel down into the whale's bones.

The worms feed on fats and oils from the bones.

Bone-eating worms have no eyes, no mouths and no stomachs.

In time, microbes spread over the whale's bones.

Then sea snails live in this microhabitat and feed on the microbes.

Whale bone

The yellow is a covering of microbes.

You Are the Microhabitat!

Did you know that on and in your body there are lots of microhabitats?

Your intestines are home to trillions of microbes.

Mouth

Stomach

Large intestine

Small intestine

Some microbes break down your food and turn it into sugars. Other microbes turn the sugars into energy for your body to use.

Your eyelashes grow from tiny openings called follicles.

Eyelash mite

Eyelashes

Each follicle is a microhabitat.

A close-up picture of a follicle.

Eyelash

Eyelash mites

Microscopic eyelash mites live in the follicles and feed on tiny pieces of dead skin.

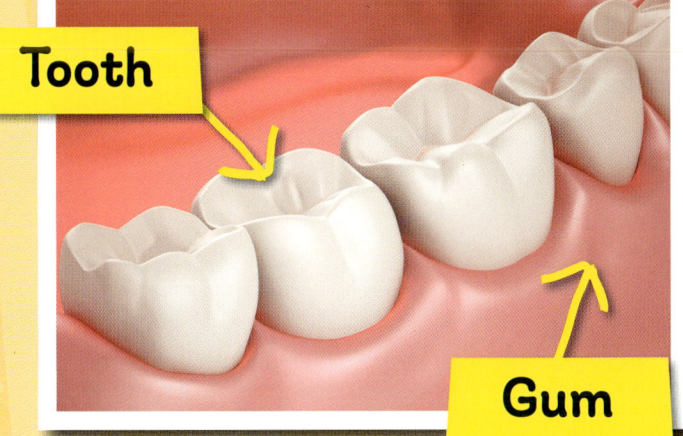

Tooth

Gum

Let's Talk

Why do you think each one of your teeth is a microhabitat?

(The answer is on page 32.)

Glossary

adapted
Changed over time to live in a particular way or a particular environment.

damp
Slightly wet.

environment
The place where living things make their home, and all the things, such as air, weather and soil, that affect them.

fungi
A group of living things that includes mushrooms, toadstools and mould.

habitat
A natural environment, for example a garden, where living things, such as animals, normally live.

larva
The young form of some animals. A caterpillar is a type of larva.

microbes
Microscopic living things. Some microbes are helpful and some, such as germs, can be harmful.

microscopic
Too small to see without a microscope.

oxygen
A gas in the air that people and animals need to breathe.

pupa
The stage in the life cycle of some insects when they change from a larva to an adult.

Index

C
compost heaps 12–13, 14–15

F
fungi 13, 18

G
gardens 4–5, 6–7, 8, 17, 19

H
human bodies 30–31, 32

L
logs 16–17, 18–19, 20

M
microbes 12, 22, 29, 30
minibeasts 6–7, 8–9, 10–11, 14–15, 16–17, 32
moss 19, 20–21

P
puddles 22–23, 32

R
rocks 7, 10, 24–25

W
whale falls 26–27, 28–29

Answers

Page 11:
Woodlice choose dark places to live to stay away from sunlight that might dry their bodies. They must stay damp so they can breathe.

Page 22:
If a puddle dries up, a rotifer dries up, too. It waits in the dry mud until more rain falls and the puddle refills. Then the rotifer takes in water and goes back to swimming and feeding.

Page 31:
Each one of your teeth is a microhabitat where microbes live. The microbes form a sticky covering called plaque that can damage your teeth. Brushing your teeth gets rid of plaque.